MW01630555

Edited by Sherie Gross

ISBN 978-1-59826-097-7

FELDHEIM PUBLISHERS
POB 43163, Jerusalem, Israel

208 Airport Executive Park
Nanuet, New York 10943

Distributed in Europe by:
LEHMANNS
+44-0-191-430-0333
info@lehmanns.co.uk
www.lehmanns.co.uk

Distributed in Australia by:
GOLDS WORLD OF JUDAICA
+613 95278775
info@golds.com.au
www.golds.com.au

Printed in Israel

For Tuvia

A.W.

FELDHEIM

Gavriel's Storm

By Aviva Werner

Illustrated by Avi Katz

My favorite thing to do after school is ride my bike.
I like to feel the sunshine on my face and the wind on my back.

But today the wind is extra strong.
Leaves and twigs swirl around the sidewalk.
Gray clouds begin to block the sunshine…
I feel a storm coming.

"Abba," I cry as I run inside. "I'm afraid."
A flash of lightning brightens the kitchen, but I don't see Abba there.

He's not in the living room or dining room either. Just as I reach the steps, I hear a clap of thunder. It rumbles and roars. My hands tremble.

"Abba!" I call. He comes. Abba helps me take off my helmet, and wraps me in his safe Abba arms. Just then a fresh ribbon of lightning streaks across the sky outside our window.

Abba says the *berachah* over lightning as he squeezes my hand.

בָּרוּךְ אַתָּה ה' אֱלֹקֵינוּ מֶלֶךְ הָעוֹלָם עֹשֶׂה מַעֲשֵׂה בְרֵאשִׁית

BLESSED ARE YOU, HASHEM, OUR G-D, KING OF THE WORLD, WHO MAKES THE WORK OF CREATION.

"I'm here, Gavriel," says Abba. "You're safe."
I squeeze his hand. Feeling Abba's closeness makes me feel calm.

"Gavriel," Abba asks, "do you know why Hashem sends us lightning?"

Abba takes down a *sefer* from the shelf. He tells me that it says in *Tehillim* that Hashem made lightning for the rain. He begins to explain.

“Rain and lightning work together to make our fruits and vegetables extra delicious and health—”

A booming crash of thunder carries Abba's words away.
The loud noise makes my heart thump in my chest.

This time we say the *berachah* over thunder together.

בָּרוּךְ אַתָּה ה' אֱלֹקֵינוּ מֶלֶךְ הָעוֹלָם שֶׁכֹּחוֹ וּגְבוּרָתוֹ מָלֵא עוֹלָם

BLESSED ARE YOU, HASHEM, OUR G-D, KING OF THE WORLD,
FOR HIS STRENGTH AND HIS POWER FILL THE WORLD.

My hands stop shaking.
I take a deep breath and the beating of my heart quiets down.

"And thunder comes from Hashem, too," Abba continues. "Do you know, Gavriel, why Hashem made thunder?"

"To wake us up?" I ask. "Kind of like the shofar?"

Abba shows me a Gemara which says that Hashem created thunder to remind us that He is more powerful than anything in the world.

"It's Hashem Who's in charge — of weather and everything else in our lives," says Abba. "The loud claps and cracks remind us of that."

I hear another rumble of thunder — in the distance this time.
I try to remember that Hashem is taking care of me and that He's in charge.

"Hashem made lightning and thunder when He created the whole world," Abba reminds me. "And He gave us the Torah with thunderous booms and flashing zips of light."

I take another deep breath. Now I hear the rain pounding on the roof in big splatters and splashes. Hashem sure knows how to get my attention.

“Hang in there, Gavriel,” says Abba. “The storm will clear soon enough. And then, if we look up to the sky, we may just see a rainbow. You know, a rainbow is also a message from Hashem. It’s a sign that Hashem remembers His promise to Noach that He will never destroy our world.”

The storm has passed and I'm back on my bike. I feel the sunshine on my face once again. The wind brushes gently against my cheeks. In the sky, the rainbow is more beautiful than ever — colorful and bright — and I know that it's a sign from Hashem to me that He's taking care of me, that He's in charge. I'm safe.

בָּרוּךְ אַתָּה ה' אֱלֹקֵינוּ מֶלֶךְ הָעוֹלָם זוֹכֵר הַבְּרִית וְנֶאֱמָן בִּבְרִיתוֹ וְקַיָּם בְּמַאֲמָרוֹ

BLESSED ARE YOU, HASHEM, OUR G-D, KING OF THE WORLD,
WHO REMEMBERS THE *BRIS*, IS TRUSTWORTHY IN HIS *BRIS*,
AND KEEPS HIS WORD.

The storm was scary,
but I have nothing to fear.

What Causes a Thunderstorm?

"He raises the clouds from the edge of the earth; He made lightning for the rain; He finds wind [to send] out of His treasuries" (Tehillim 135:7).

"Thunder was created to straighten out the crookedness of one's heart" (Berachos 59a).

Air is constantly on the move. Hot air rises up, while warm air sinks down. All of this movement creates wind. When wind picks up water vapor from the ground, it carries the vapor up into the sky. The air gets cooler as it rises higher, and the water vapor that it is carrying forms into clouds. As the air rises higher still, the vapor freezes, forming ice.

Ice is heavy, and the ice from the clouds eventually falls back down to the ground. If it falls slowly, it has time to melt as it passes through warmer air and comes down as rain. If it falls quickly, hail hits the ground. But when the ice and water particles inside a cloud bump into and rub against each other, they create electric charges.

When these electric charges become too strong, pressure builds inside the cloud. A bolt of lightning releases this pressure, connecting with electrical charges on the ground. Lightning heats up the air around the bolt to super-hot temperatures — even hotter than the surface of the sun.

Because hot air takes up more space than cold air, the super-heated air around the bolt expands very quickly. It forcefully pushes aside the air next to it, causing the air to vibrate. We hear these vibrations as the sound of thunder. Light moves faster than sound, which is why we see lightning before we hear its thunder.

When lightning streaks across the sky, its intense heat causes chemical reactions that change nitrogen gases in the air into nitrates. These nitrates then fall to the ground with the rain, where they mix in with the soil. They are a key ingredient in plant fertilizer. Thunderstorms also clean the air, bring down temperatures on a hot day, and deliver much-needed water to people, plants, and rivers.

Here's how Gavriel's father helped his son overcome fear of lightning and thunder. Use these tips to help your child cope during a thunderstorm, too.

1. **Validate your child's fears.** Loud noises can be scary, and flashes of light can be unexpected and unsettling. Because thunderstorms are loud, startling and potentially dangerous, most children (and many adults, too) find them terrifying. Tell your child that you understand why he is scared. If you were afraid of thunder when you were a child, share this with him. Don't expect him to be a "big boy" and don't tell him he's being silly or childish for being afraid.

2. **Create a safe place for your child** to weather the storm. Give her plenty of hugs and other comforting forms of physical contact, such as hand-holding or cuddling. She might feel most secure in her bed, in a parent's or sibling's bed, or inside a couch-cushion fort of her own creation.

3. **Help your child stay calm** by taking deep breaths. Show him how to

inhale (breathe in) slowly through his nose, hold his breath for a few seconds, then exhale (breathe out) slowly through his mouth. Do this deep-breathing exercise along with your child. After four breaths like this, he should feel calmer.

4. **Explain what's happening outside** and why. Understanding the science behind lightning and thunder can make these natural phenomena less frightening. And understanding why Hashem created lightning and thunder gives the phenomena meaning and purpose. Use the explanation on the previous pages to guide the discussion.

5. **Recite the appropriate *berachos***. Teach your child to turn to Hashem in times of fear and to trust in Hashem always. The *berachos* upon seeing lightning and hearing thunder should be recited within a second or two of seeing a flash of lightning or hearing a thunder clap, and may only be recited once per storm. When reciting the *berachah* upon seeing a rainbow, make sure to only look at the rainbow, not stare at it.